Finding My Way

Finding My Way

A Journey Along the Rim of the
Catholic Worker Movement

Toni Flynn

SAND RIVER PRESS
Los Osos, California

Published by Sand River Press, 1319 14th Street, Los Osos, CA 93402.

Copies of this book may be obtained by sending $7.95, plus $1.50 postage and handling to the above address. CALIFORNIA RESIDENTS PLEASE ADD 6% sales tax.

Copies of this book may also be obtained by sending the above amounts to the Los Angeles Catholic Worker, 632 N. Brittania Street, Los Angeles, CA 90033.

The contents of this collection originally appeared in editions of the *Catholic Agitator*. Some of the articles were subsequently reprinted in *The Other Side Magazine*.

First Printing

10 9 8 7 6 5 4 3 2 1

ISBN 0-944627-33-1

Printed in the United States of America.

CONTENTS

BOOK 1: FRAGILE LEGACY

BOOK 2: ENCOUNTERS

BOOK 3: BEYOND THE REEF

For My Children

David

Mark

Shannon

Heather

FOREWORD

Dorothy Day writes at the beginning of her autobiography, *The Long Loneliness:*
> *Going to confession is hard. Writing a book*
> *is hard, because you are "giving yourself away."*
> *But if you love you want to give yourself.*

For the past several years, Toni Flynn has recklessly and lovingly given herself away in the pages of *The Catholic Agitator.* As an editor of that paper, I've had the opportunity of watching Toni perform the difficult work of translating truthful emotion and experience into plain English. At times I've wondered if she were being too honest—I would gasp, "My God, you can't say this. These people are still alive!" The impulse to broadcast the minutiae of one's life in print can also indicate a bad case of narcissism. Yet, to my mind, Toni's expeditions into herself are not *self*ish, but rather a way of living in the truth, and, ultimately, a way of authentically evangelizing others. Dorothy Day explains, "You write about yourself because in the long run all our problems are the same, the same human needs of sustenance and love."

Toni belongs to the literary genre of modern confessionalism, whose leading figure is the poet Robert Lowell. Toni, like Lowell, addresses public events through events of the mind. Lowell once documented his attendance at a Vietnam War protest by talking about his "leg- and arch-cramps" and "cowardly foolhardy heart." That sounds like Toni.

But why, then, publish someone's private journal in a radical newspaper like *The Agitator?* This is just the point. What distinguishes today's religious peace and justice movement from those in the past is the recognition that political conversion is not enough. Knowing the facts or thinking the right thoughts does not necessarily change the individual—witness the fact that the United States is presently engaged in preparing for nuclear war, potentially the worst crime in human history, and yet so few Americans respond to this reality as an urgent moral problem. What immobilizes us then is not the *fact* of our sinfulness (did it ever?) but fear of facing who we've become, and the spectre of responsibility that accompanies this knowledge. Toni opens that hardened box where we keep all those "things" we really don't want to talk about, those hurts and doubts that we believe are tangential to our more important work of peacemaking—those painful experiences that have convinced us that a heart of flesh is too thin a vault to keep in the bad neighborhood of this world. Her writing embodies an important question: how are we ever to become truly committed in our whole being, freely willing to turn away from the dominant, wealthy, and violent culture, if all we have going for us are the *right* words, *right* beliefs, and *right* membership? We righteous ones are in need of conversion, of being freed from orthodoxy as much as those on the Right. We need people like Toni Flynn to remind us of our hypocrisy.

Just as going to confession is hard, taking in Toni's words can be difficult. Inadequacies and screw-ups and terrible sins of omission surface to consciousness. Yet, in the end, we believe we are forgiven, always forgiven. This is the sacrament of reconciliation: to be made human again, reconciled with God, with others, with ourselves.

Jonathan Parfrey

ACKNOWLEDGEMENTS

Grateful acknowledgement to the many Los Angeles Catholic Worker community members (past and present) who have accepted me in my contradictions, motivated me to write down my struggles, and inspired me with their radical vision of peace, compassion and justice rooted in spirituality.

In particular, to Ray Correio, who said of the first article I ever submitted to *The Agitator*, "Needs work, but show Jeff." To Jeff Dietrich, who (one dozen drafts later) said, "If Joan likes it, we'll print it." To Joan Trafecanty who said, "I like it!" Also to Jonathan Parfrey who over the years has persistently interrupted our conversations with ". . .now *that* would make a great article in the next *Agitator* issue!"

Although there are no specific stories written about them in this book, I would also like to mention three of the most unforgettable friends I've ever met who have influenced my life (and therefore, my writing) beyond explanation and who together encompass the widest spectrum of Catholic Workerism: Chris Cowles, Eugene Fejnas and Eddy O'Brien.

Deep appreciation to all the following: Christa Occhiogrosso, artist and soulmate, whose illustrations grace this book with beauty and substance; Gary Wheeler-Cavalier, Joan Trafecanty, John Peter Lathourakis, and Bruce Miller, each of whom contributed to making the publication of this book possible.

And finally, loving gratitude to Chris O'Connell who has relentlessly encouraged me in finding my way. . .

AUTHOR'S PREFACE

Dorothy Day (1897-1980) founded the Catholic Worker in New York in 1933 as an independent lay Catholic movement committed to living out the Works of Mercy by serving the poor through houses of hospitality and soup kitchens. Catholic Workers are pacifists and hold that war and violence are contrary to the teachings of the Gospel. There are now over 80 Worker houses throughout the U.S. and in other countries.

Dorothy Day has been called a modern saint by many. Fortunately for me, she was also a woman who experienced many seemingly contradictory phases in her lifetime, and it was because of her humanness that I felt drawn to her work. More than ten years ago, in the throes of my divorce, I tiptoed timidly onto the rim of the Catholic Worker movement by chopping onions for a day at the Los Angeles community's soup kitchen on skid row. I was at the time what might be described as a "mass of contradictions"!

A few years later, still chopping onions and still a mass of contradictions, I began writing and publishing reflections about my struggles in the L.A. Catholic Worker newspaper, *The Agitator*.

The collection of articles in this book were written and published in *The Agitator* over a seven-year period (1982-1988), during which time I lived with my children in California in both Los Angeles and San Luis Obispo counties.

The articles are printed in order of theme rather than chronologically and encompass stories about everything from the onions to the contradictions! The names and identifiable characteristics of some of the people appearing in the

AUTHOR'S PREFACE

"Encounters" and "Beyond the Reef" stories were altered to protect their anonymity.

People have asked me why I never actually "joined" the L.A. Catholic Worker community. The truth is that I have no ready answer to that question other than to comment that my continuous journey around the rim of the Worker movement has been transformational—and has, if nothing else, brought me to the brink of my own social conscience and close to the center of my soul.

INTRODUCTION

One of the more hidden facts about Toni Flynn is that, as a perky, well-groomed California teenager in the early sixties, perhaps to compensate for a less-than-idyllic childhood, she became a pom-pom girl on the high school drill team. Later she married a high school football hero turned police officer and moved into a condominium in the San Fernando Valley, complete with swimming pool, to live the comfortable, insulated middle class lifestyle to which perky cheerleader types are bred.

Though the Barbie-and-Ken fantasy never quite worked out for Toni, there was still a lot of the gushing ingenue in the first manuscript that she submitted to *The Catholic Agitator.* The pages fairly dripped with the sticky syrup of her saccharine prose. Golden sunsets, daisies on the hill, and even "happily-ever-after" dotted her writing like the sugary flowers on a child's baroque birthday cake.

But there was a paragraph about a homeless man and a statue of the Infant of Prague that reached out from the pages and grabbed me like a meat-hook, preventing me from tossing the whole thing into the round file. I covered the margins with red lines and rude comments and sent it back to her in the certainty that I had intimidated this pretentious cheerleader from ever approaching a typewriter again, much less a busy editor.

Fortunately, I had underestimated Toni's desire to write and overestimated my ability to intimidate her. A dozen rewrites (on her part) and 500 rude comments (on my part) later, *The Catholic Agitator* had the privilege to be the first publication to print an article by Toni Flynn.

INTRODUCTION

Toni's struggle as a writer to make that transition from a superficial, childish prose style to a child-like, but authentic, vision of the world reflects the broader struggle of her life in its journey from the comfortable coffee clatches and Tupperware parties of her young adulthood to the darker landscapes of Los Angeles' skid row, the locked wards of Atascadero State Hospital for the criminally insane where she worked as a psychiatric technician, and the blockade lines at the Diablo Canyon Nuclear Power Plant.

This is a journey inspired and sustained by faith. It has nothing to do with the current journalistic fetish for the bizarre and the misanthropic. Rather, it is based on the recognition that the reality of the world involves the reality of suffering. Thus, to live authentically and to write authentically is to be in touch with that suffering reality.

I am grateful, as I am certain you will be too, that Toni has chosen to bring us along on that journey.

Jeff Dietrich

BOOK 1
FRAGILE LEGACY

I used to question stars and books, but I have begun to listen to the teachings my blood whispers to me. My story is not a pleasant one; it is neither sweet nor harmonious as invented stories are; it has the taste of nonsense and chaos, of madness and dreams—like the lives of those who stop deceiving themselves.

—Herman Hesse

GROWING UP CATHOLIC

s it necessary to explain that, as a little girl I hero-worshipped both my father and my Catholic faith? Because of this, I cannot speak about growing up Catholic unless I also speak about my father. He was raised by Italian-Catholic parents in the old-country tradition. The youngest child, he was spoiled by his mother. Growing up the son of immigrants at the turn of the century in a small, midwestern Protestant town, he was systematically targeted with ripe tomatoes and ethnic slurs by the "regular boys" while on his way to serve daily Mass as an altar boy in his neighborhood church.

He survived the persecution of both the tomatoes and the name-calling and grew into a man of depth, character, and contradictions—a man whose passions eventually ran away with him like a team of horses in one of those old Western movies, racing and pulling their covered-wagon helter-skelter across some dusty frontier plain.

Relatives tell me that my father had ambitions in his youth of becoming a lawyer or a priest. But by the time he married my Irish mother and fathered me, he was a fast-dealing used car salesman, deep into middle age and deeper still into the bottle. Prone to violent outbursts at night, he lived by day on a diet of dreams, alcohol, and atonement.

When I reached school age, he no longer practiced Catholicism or any other formal religion. It remains an enigma to me exactly how and why he persevered in providing for me to attend a very well-established and prestigious Catholic school in Santa Monica. I have no idea where the tuition money came from, since he worked at the used car lot maybe six months out of any given year, frequenting local taverns for "prospective auto buyers" the other six, charming everyone who occupied a barstool with his humor and his melancholy.

I know this because I used to accompany him as a very young child. "My daughter is the best girl God ever put breath into," he would boast to his inebriated audiences. "She goes to Catholic school and she's going to be better than her old man." This was my cue to curtsy politely, holding the hem of my blue organdy party dress and pointing a black patent-leather toe just so. I would then sing a selection of "Blessed Mother" songs, thereby reducing everyone to tears and collecting from them assorted small change left over from bartender tips. If my father cried audibly and visibly, I received additional barrages of fifty-cent pieces and a few dollar bills. In this way, my father and I teamed up, earning me my hot school lunches.

Catholic school and Church served as my sanctuary from

the harsher realities of my unpredictable, chaotic home life. I can still see, feel, smell, taste and hear the Catholic Church I romanticized in my youth...the figure of Sister Mary Oliver towering benevolently over my first-grade desk in her long black woolen robes, smelling of perspiration and baby powder, her hair tucked tidily under a tailored, starched veil with her rosary beads clickety-clicking around her waist...Holy Mass in a church filled with plaster figures of Mary, Joseph, and saints too numerous to name, let alone remember, multitudes of lighted candles, flat bread and purple wine mysteriously transformed into Jesus through the soft, undecipherable, ancient prose of the priest...a curtained box, me on my skinned-up skinny knees doing my confession to a shadow person who spoke to God about my sins—the God who was perfect and powerful enough to forgive or withhold forgiveness...Jesus on the cross above the altar with red blood painted on His hands and feet and side, perpetually dying for love of me...*Panis Angelicus* and *Ave Maria* floating up above an old pipe organ's hum...little blue and white Catechism books telling me how to follow rules that would indeed make me the "better girl" my father desired.

And so I grew up "Catholic" and "good." For most of the years of my adult life, it remained essential for me to continue to see my father only in terms of his goodness and his sadness—a man burdened and frustrated by his unrealized potential, but otherwise faultless. I repressed most memories of my father's drinking and the resultant domestic violence pervasive in our home, experiencing it only in forms of vague flash-back images that appeared and disappeared at random, stress-filled periods.

It was equally important for me to continue to view the

3

Catholic Church (my father's one consistently stable gift to me) through proverbial rose-colored glasses, thereby preserving for myself a secure, protective, innocent corner of faith in a seemingly faithless, hostile world that I could not otherwise trust. I would not allow anyone to criticize "my" Church in any way. I refused to listen when people challenged the Church on issues of abuse of power, over-accumulation of wealth and property, the status of women, the unmet needs of the poor, the comfortable conventionality of some suburban parishes. I was only able to acknowledge the validity of these concerns to some degree when I became involved with the Catholic Worker Community. Why? Because I sublimated my hero-worship of the Church in general in order to idealize the more specific Catholic Worker Movement. Any community that worked so diligently for social justice, world peace, and the poor, was nearly perfect! Once again, I abstained from a more critical acceptance of a struggling community, and felt instead only the need to attach myself to a vision of the ideal.

It may or may not have been possible for me to hold back for a lifetime any authentic confrontation with reality concerning my past and my present human condition and my spiritual life. But there are those moments, I think, for all of us, when we are presented with the opportunity to tear down the hundred delusions and illustrations we have invented to protect ourselves from the truth. I believe it is only with some mystical combination of grace and courage that these moments are acted upon and effect the beginning of transformation in our lives.

For me, those opportune moments came and went and I chose to let them go, repeating old self-deceptions rather than

4 ·

risk coming to terms with awful truths that might force me to reject my father, abandon my faith, and, in fact, lose my entire identity.

Finally, some years ago, I was granted one more opportunity. My father, proving himself fallible after all, grew old and ill and died quietly in the end. I stood in the twilight at his grave-site for what seemed like hours after the funeral service ended, thinking and watching the wind scatter leaves aimlessly off of trees, mocking the order of well-positioned tombstones. I asked myself if I could face in his death that which I could not face during his life...that he was a bad man and that he was a good man and that the two were inseparable. Slowly, ever so slowly, I let myself go out to my father's reality, seeing him as a man of incredible strength and of equally incredible weakness. I relived some of the terrible times with him and some of the golden ones. I called him a bastard and cried out that I loved him. I looked down at the dirt that covered him, smelling the pungent fragrance of freshly-turned damp sod, and I recognized that he had loved me in extreme imperfection but nonetheless, he had given me his love.

That evening, I felt as though I had been released from a chain of fantasies that had served as survival tools in my childhood but that had dragged me down all of my adult life— always having feared that if I did not perceive someone (even my own self) or something as all good, they would prove to be all bad, thus subjecting me to abandonment and lostness in some great interior void. With growing awareness over the next few months, I began to review all that I held precious—my father, my relationships, my Church, the world, my own soul—in terms of a woven pattern, whereby flaws and discolorations are integral to the whole.

With a fragile sense of liberation, I have lived these past few years trying to reconcile myself to truth, leaving fantasy behind. It is not easy for me. My spiritual life is tainted more often now with fears, doubt, confusion. Though more critical, I still consider myself a Catholic. I still celebrate Mass and I marvel at the life of Christ as told in the Gospels, connecting His journey even more intensely with my own. I have remained involved with the Catholic Worker, only now I allow myself to see the fuller, more human picture of their community struggles and how that intertwines with the genuinely valuable work they accomplish.

I can now acknowledge that I will find no corner on earth, no church, no family, no community, no person who is exempt from darkness. Paradoxically, this gives me more hope to continue to live in a world still bent on war and injustice, because I can now believe that acknowledging the darkness does not negate the light. Working in the mental health field with mentally disturbed men, women, children, confirms this to me over and over again, since I have yet to experience a patient— even the most severely emotionally damaged—who does not have some periods of lucidity, however brief.

By no means am I completely "transformed." I hesitate to mention the frequency of my own instances of insanity so subtly mingled with moments of balance and grace...those times when I feel incapable of authenticity, productivity, or any form of intimacy. As a result, I suffer through long bouts of depression when I am tempted to slip back into the safer, more familiar isolation of my old illusions where only heroes and villains exist.

But during my more contemplative moments, I find myself asking if perhaps the immense Light that is God's own Love, casts an equivalently immense shadow. I realize this question poses far-reaching theological implications since we normally associate "shadows" and "darkness" with those destructive dimensions of ourselves and of the world that we try so hard to conceal, justify, or deny. Yet the question remains one I dare to ask myself. For is it not the concealment, justifications, and denials, rather than the shadow itself, that conceive and perpetuate destruction? This has proven true in my own life. And when I search my heart for a God who is meaningful to me in my own truth today, I meet a God who is experiencially conscious of both Love and shadow, a God who most tenderly and intimately embraces all of us as we struggle to weave together our darkness and our light.

WOMAN AT THE WELL

ere I to tell the full story about my wedding (a 65-minute Latin Mass with two priests), my marriage (10 years with four resulting children), and my divorce (five minutes in a courtroom with a lawyer and a judge), it would read like a poorly scripted B movie. The decline and fall of human commitment repeats itself monotonously from case to case, and though my own holds elements of the tragic, it would prove nonetheless boring and embarassing in print. What I want to write about instead is my lack of experience with the mystery of relationship and how my own journey into that mystery began paradoxically with the process Catholics know as the marriage annulment.

I had been divorced for over five years before I really moved my life in any sort of healing direction. During those years I bore a tremendous load of guilt and resentment. (Dare I admit to reveling in the burden?) I became expert at pointing blame. After all, I reasoned with one-dimensional accuracy, my marriage had been escape from, reaction against, perpetuation of inherited unhealthy family patterns. It was compounded, I further rationalized, with my Catholic education in the sixties which advocated that young "good" girls maintain their virginal

9

innocence (i.e. ignorance, naivete) until after their wedding vows, from which moment on they must miraculously and immediately acquire profound maturity and wisdom as women, wives, and mothers of several baptized children.

In short, I blamed entirely my parents, my former husband, and my Church for the failure of my marriage. As for my part, mingled with the bitterness, I was of course remorseful...and chronically, unforgivingly penitent for the choices that rendered me the blameless victim. In this way I suffered. But it was a sterile suffering, recycling itself through the same old patterns rather than moving in a direction indicating growth, transformation.

There is a wonderful scene in a recent movie "The Mission" where Robert de Niro (a mercenary and a murderer) literally carries all of his heavy armor and weaponry in a net on his back as he painfully makes his way up a steep, muddy cliff. For five years I carried my emotional weaponry around and admittedly, a certain security accompanied the burden. So long as I carried it, there was no need to look at it, sort it out, surrender it. And so my "junk" followed me out of my marriage and into relationship after relationship, with me always concluding that the *other* person betrayed my attempts to relate. It seemed I learned nothing, gained nothing. I grew exceedingly lonely.

Grace has a way of falling and hitting me over the head when I least expect it. One Sunday, I came across two passages— one in scripture where Jesus spends time with the woman at the well (you know, the one who had trouble remembering how many men she had in her life!) I interpreted, *not* that Jesus confronted her, so much as that he accepted her in all of her entanglements, and helped her to confront herself. She disclosed

10

to her friends exultantly, "Come and see someone who told me everything I did!" It was her moment of liberation. The other reading was from a book by Ranier Maria Rilke about "that dangerous insecurity that is so much more human than security; that drives prisoners to feel out the shapes of their horrible dungeons and not be strangers to the unspeakable terror of their abode."

I began to feel a hunger...a desire to take the lid off of the soup pot of my relationships. To taste and see what simmered and boiled inside—what devils were bubbling under the surface. To call them by their proper names. Confront them. Admit to them. Embrace them as my own and to hope for redemption from them. To do this, I turned ironically to my Church. Perhaps re-turned is the more proper way to describe it. I petitioned for an annulment from the very Church towards which I still felt a great deal of ambivalence.

Canonically, the Catholic Church will grant an annulment if it is deemed that the relationship was not a binding sacramental marriage—either something was seriously lacking in how or why the decision was made to get married or one or both persons were incapable of fulfilling "a Christian Marriage" (even though they may have entered it in good faith at the time). Vatican II defines "Christian Marriage" as "an intimate community of love and life."

At the time I petitioned, it wasn't so important to me whether or not I would be granted the formal annulment based on any of those terms. It was the process itself I desired. The process of delving, questioning, exploring my patterns of intimacy (or lack of) in my relationships. I wanted to begin to take on some personal responsibility for my life, its failures and

11

its strengths. I wanted to take the risk of discovering whether or not I could fathom the meaning of love and commitment on any level. For weeks I sweated over the 50 or 60 questions on the petition, probing into my heart and soul as I had never done before. I met the devils within—festering in the soup pot—in the form of deceptions, distortions, delusions and illusions. I discovered I knew almost nothing about authentic intimacy and I was terrified of commitment. Relationship for me was synonymous with sickness.

Rilke also wrote, "If there is anything morbid in your processes, just remember that sickness is the means by which an organism frees itself of foreign matter, so one must help it to have its whole sickness and break out with it, for that is progress." For me the annulment process was a purgation, an act of purification. I took it seriously. Why? I hesitate to draw simplistic conclusions. What I can say is that going through the annulment procedure felt more sacramental to me than did my marriage ceremony.

In the end, I was granted an annulment. I suppose I am glad for this. What I am more grateful for is to be part of a Church that, despite what I consider drawbacks and flaws in some of its teachings, provided a way for me to integrate, heal, reconcile myself with myself. I don't know if I can say that my ability to sustain relationships has deepened, grown enormously. But I know that I have a new vision of what committed intimacy should be: Each person reveals to the other what's bubbling in the pot—devils and all. Each greets the other, liberates the other, respects the solitariness of the other. Each calls the other into the mystery of intimacy and outward to the challenge of restoring peace and integrity in our broken world. Each stands on the rim

12

of the other's soul, looking in and marvelling at the intricately balanced design of shadows and light that compose a human life. In my own ungraceful, yet grace-filled way, I'm getting there.

MY SON MARK ON HIS 12th BIRTHDAY

ne of the advantages of small town living is that no event is too insignificant to celebrate. Having been a divorced mother of four for nearly six years, I've grown used to participating in most of these provincial festivities as "not quite" a complete family unit.

Once in a while, however, a longtime friend travels up from L.A. to spend a weekend with us, and we do seem to form a natural sort of fatherly/motherly relationship with my children for the duration of his stay. This time—late September—my second son's birthday was an occasion for such a visit. My friend drove up and met us at the Annual Harvest Festival—a local day of celebration which my son, Mark, had chosen for us to attend as a fitting way to welcome his twelfth year.

When we arrived at mid-morning, the town square (yes, we have a genuine, old-fashioned town square) was already swarming with folks buzzing in and about the various game booths, food concession stands, arts and crafts displays. As we walked through the entrance, Mark paused and glanced toward a nearby corner at what must have been no small spectacle for a boy just turned twelve years old. An actual army set-up— complete with American flag, a chow truck, two jeeps, a tank and

15

assorted weaponry—was accented by the vigilance of five strapping young army recruits, dressed in combat fatigues, their hair well-shorn, boots spit-polished. The soldiers offered my son some K-ration samples, but I nervously pulled him along with me. Time enough to worry about the possibility of such things when he approaches eighteen. Not this birthday. Not yet.

The day waned as the Indian Summer sun poured down on us, casting a honey-haze over the gazebo where the six of us now stood chomping on corn-dogs dipped in mustard, listening to a barber shop quartet drone on about the harvest moon shining for somebody and his gal. It was a fine family outing until the crowd grew in such proportions as to give the most mentally sound person a case of claustrophobia. The noise level reached chaotic heights as well. It was time to go home. As we pushed through the crowd to our separate cars, I thought I heard my companion say he would take Mark with him, so I grabbed up the three remaining youngsters and made a dash for the parking lot.

We reached the house where my friend was already sitting in the rocker reading the evening paper. "Where's Mark?" he questioned. My heart skipped a beat. "I thought he was with you." Oh, great! We had inadvertently left the birthday boy to the mercy of the harvest festing throngs. We made an agreement. The others would remain home in case Mark some- how showed up on his own. I would return to the Festival to try and find him among the masses.

It seemed an impossible task. In a town of 10,000, I estimated that every last resident, down to the most sickly and infirm, had managed to cram themselves into this one spot. I searched for two hours, calling home at intervals. The sharp edge of a sickening panic crept in toward my stomach lining. My mind played the old "what if" trick on me—what if he ran away . . . got lost . . . hit by a car . . . kidnapped . . . was drowned in the creek . . . molested . . . beaten up . . . food-poisoned . . . ?

Suddenly, I remembered the U.S. Army and the K-rations. I ran back toward the entrance and, sure enough, there he was, parked on a wooden crate, resting his arm on a machine gun of some kind or another, eating yellow pastey looking stuff out of a can. "That's my son!" I yelled venomously at the young men in their camouflage fighting fatigues as though they had done Mark great harm. Jerking him away by the arm, I began to cry. "Where have you been? I've spent hours looking for you. Don't you know how worried we all were? Why are you *here* of all places?" Mark had no defense against my hysterical ranting and raving.

It was not until the next day, that I felt calm enough to communicate effectively. I took Mark alone with me to the beach for a talk. "Why, Mark? Why was it so important for you to spend so much time with those soldiers?" Mark sat down on the sand, quietly, reflectively. The salty air grew so still that I could hear the flapping of the gulls' wings as they skimmed across the white caps. Finally, he spoke. "At first, I wanted to find out what army food tasted like. Ya know . . . to see if it was different. Then I started talking to the soldiers, and I had to stay."

Once again, silence. This time a dog strolled by and I heard his panting—rhythmical and wet-sounding—in line with his pace and the saliva drooling from his mouth. Mark began again. "Mom, I had to ask them about their guns. I wanted to know why they had to use them. They told me it was so that they could protect our country from being hurt. I thought and thought. Then I looked at them and said that if I ever had to use

17

one of those guns to kill someone, I guess I'd hurt forever—so our country would still have hurt in it."

More silence. I heard myself swallow. It sounded like thunder in my throat. "Mark, what did they reply to you?" "Nothing, Mom. They were quiet."

I looked at my boy as he stood up. He appeared so strangely whole to me. His slight frame was poised un-self-consciously, like the open palm of a monk at prayer, serene and accepting, at one with the sand and sea. I put my hand on his shoulder and we walked along the shore, our steps mimicking the flap, flap of the sea gulls' wings. Anyone happening to look at us at that moment could have seen that (much like the birds overhead) we were in miraculous flight.

IN MEMORIAM: A FRAGILE LEGACY

he five of us formed a procession through the cemetery in the middle of our small town. Heather, my
youngest child, in the lead, the three others in close
pursuit. I was trailing behind reflectively when David stopped in
his tracks, calling out, "I think this is the row, Mom. I remember
last year, we found them by a sprinkler spout." Mark and
Shannon, in their youthful exuberance, reminded us to look for
the whitest stones because "last year we washed them,
remember?" Up one row, down another, I guessed we had
miscalculated our precise destination when suddenly they were
before us—Reynaldo and Donald. "Our soldiers! We found our
soldiers!" Heather was already kneeling in front of their
tombstones, running her tiny fingers over letters spelling out the
final poetry of their lives: SP, Co. C, 47 INF., 9th INF. DIV.,
Vietnam, and SP 4, Co. C, 6th BN., 9th INF. DIV., Vietnam.
"What do all those letters mean?" she asked, then continued her
fingerplay over more understandable data: Nov. 26, 1946-May
15, 1967, and May 7, 1947-Sept. 1, 1967. "I know what that
means, Mom. It means they were born and they died." Our
annual Memorial Day ritual was underway.

These visits had begun when we moved to Grover City a

19

few years ago from Los Angeles. I confess, it was not a patriotic act on my part. It was more a gesture of kindness that had grown out of a promise to a friend who had graduated from high school with the two boys who were buried here. "I will remember them," I had said. The original intention had been to "remember" them with one visit, but inexplicably, I found myself returning year after year. This time, we pulled up weeds threatening to choke the color portrait of Reynaldo in his full dress uniform, his dark, handsome eyes and angular cheekbones barely visible under a glaze of dust and dew that had settled on the marble memorial. "Let's sing that song," requested the brood, "the one from *your* day, Mom . . . the one people sang during *your* war. And tell us about *your* soldiers."

My face reddened. This was never easy for me. How to tell my children about the controversy over "my day," "my war," "my soldiers," as though an entire era could belong to me in particular! I began anyway, speaking haltingly in simple syllables, partly to be understood by the children, partly to hide the remnants of my own bewilderment about that time in my life. "While I was busy having all of you, our country was involved in a war far away in a place called Vietnam. Many of the boys I went to high school with, fought over there, believing it to be their moral duty. Some suffered injuries. Some died. Some others refused to fight at all, believing that decision to be their moral duty. They too suffered. It was a sad time filled with confusion and conflict. There were angry demonstrations, divided feelings. Many people asked disturbing questions of themselves and of this country."

Silence. A cough or two. A deep sigh. "You forgot to do the *song*, Mom." Song? I reminded myself that "the song" had been too prosaic, even back in the sixties, and would now sound tired and out-dated. "No singing today." Instead, Shannon placed some tenderly gathered flowers on both graves while Mark offered a little prayer and Heather litanied "Peace." Only David stood back self-consciously, pretending indifference. I wondered about *his* thoughts—a boy of 15. The two boys marked here had lived only a few short years past that age—neither one of them surviving to his 21st year. "How old would Reynaldo and Donald be now?" he asked, penetrating my mind. I paused for a suspended moment. "About as old as I am." And another question, thrown at me like a dart, "If you don't believe in war, why do you bring us here every year? This is a military holiday." No available answer.

I brushed the children aside with a brisk motion, thrusting a quarter into each of their palms, bribing them across the street to buy a treat. Of course, it worked. In the blink of an eye, they were outside the cemetery gates and inside the 7-11 Store. Finally alone, my tears burst out like water from behind a weakened wall. I have the damnedest time trying to "pass on peace" to my children! How to convey the "strength" of convictions that often shake and quiver with doubt and fear inside of me? How to teach them peacemaking skills when I have not yet mastered them myself? It would be easier to flow with the patriotic stream. Easier on me—and on the children.

In this small, agricultural town, where so many genuinely good-hearted people still reap the fruits of their labor by the sweat of their brow, the old-fashioned American ethic is still gospel. Good citizens rally unquestioningly behind their President in times of crises. Good parents proudly endorse their sons over to the military. Good sons bravely sacrifice their lives to whatever current cause the U.S. government determines is just. Loyalty, honor, courage. Honed by the Red, White and Blue. Who can argue such qualities?

My personal beliefs make for suspicious speculation here. They are often interpreted as contradictions to old and revered values. If I am opposed to war, then am I also opposed to freedom? If I question and sometimes oppose the policies of my own government, then am I supportive of Communism? If I oppose the draft, then do I not care about the young men who are sent away to fight and die for the preservation of my security? I have been challenged many times by people whom I respect and would like to call my friends. A few times I have felt the wrath of man-made judgment day upon me. I understand their perspectives. Still, it is painful, for they do not seem to understand mine.

And so each year, I pack up my kids and my ideals like a refugee with no home for my dreams in this land of dreams. I hold vigil with "my soldiers" for awhile, hoping that my children will gain a few insights by witnessing the uncertain tenacity of their "flower generation" mother. There is tension—the tension of a peace person in a military cemetery balancing between respect for the sacrifice made by young soldiers who have already given up their lives, and the hope that the next generation (four of whom are sprung from my own womb) will find less violent, more lasting ways to resolve the conflict. As now, there were so many questions and no simple answers back in the sixties. I have long since discarded my flowered head-bands and wooden beads, symbols for me of that turbulent time. But I've salvaged a few seeds of perspective that were planted back then. I want so much to pass them on to my sons and daughters so that they might

IN MEMORIAM: A FRAGILE LEGACY

cultivate visions of a peaceful lifestyle that reaches beyond the markings on these tombstones and the fragility of my own attempt to live by my convictions.

The sun was beginning to set, and I could see the children waiting for me across the street. It was time to turn and walk away, leaving behind only some flowers on a couple of young men's graves and these few personal reflections. But I held back on an impulse, thinking, "What the hell! No one is listening." I suppose I reeked of childish whim and ridiculous melodrama, but here I was, standing in front of Reynaldo and Donald, contributing one final archaic question in the form of a slightly edited, very off-key, but utterly sincere version of "the song":

> *Where have all the soldiers gone?*
> *Long time passing . . .*
> *Where have all the soldiers gone?*
> *Long time ago . . .*

STAINED GLASS: PUTTING THE PIECES TOGETHER

My future lacks clarity as I drive past a city not sharply in focus, whirring along the Harbor Freeway toward the Los Angeles Catholic Worker on Sixth and Gladys Streets. I estimate this is about my sixtieth 200-mile trek to L.A.'s Skid Row since I moved to San Luis Obispo County five years ago.

Today I'm going to scrub trays and spoons at the Hospitality Kitchen, then apply for work at a hospital in Santa Monica and try to find an apartment near the beach cheap enough to get by and large enough to hold my four kids and me. I want to move back to Los Angeles. I want to spend more time on Skid Row. Friends think I'm nuts. "What about the children?" they say. The freeway traffic slows and I breathe in a little smog. Images of my sons and daughters rise up visibly before me like fragments of stained glass and I am surprised by the brilliance of their hues.

DAVID. I see him handsome and lean at 16, yet wary and always at a safe distance from me, like the color blue. He has experienced me as one experiences an ever-changing chameleon. He has survived my frailty, my pretenses, my inconsistencies. In his early years, I was an upstanding example of Christian motherhood. In terms of literal commandment-keeping and fundamental church-and-country law-abiding, I was above reproach. David was formed inside my womb when I was a young

25

insecure girl-woman trying to compensate for my own chaotic childhood by living as the "perfect" wife, mother, Catholic. With desperate determination I gave him birth, dressed him in little sailor outfits, polished his shoes, housed him in a cookie-cutter condominium complex. He was driven to swim lessons in a powder-blue luxury wagon, placed in the finest of Catholic schools, carted off to Mass every Sunday to a front row pew where I cooly displayed him to the parishioners like a piece of fine china on display in a curio cabinet.

    What his father and I lacked in the reality of our marriage, I compensated for by creating "perfect family" fantasies and serving them up to David and me. Then came the other children, disillusionment, divorce, despair, and a crash course in basic survival. My oldest child, surveyor of my past mistakes, is a respecter of the spaces needed in water and sky; our relationship is stained now an even more intense shade of blue...

    The cars are bumper to bumper now. I hope I make it to the soup kitchen too late to chop onions, but in time to slice tomatoes. I press down on the car brakes and my memory rotates upside down, then right side up.

    MARK. He tumbled from my body, shaking my life like a boulder bolting from a mountain in an earthquake. At first camouflaged as a sorrowful mystery, he has grown into a living flame burning like a steady red substance in my heart. I know him like a botanist knows the underside of a tender leaf, but it wasn't always that way. "He's not quite right," the pediatrician pronounced after Mark's three-month visit. The doctor articulated professorially the outrageous conditions my baby possessed, speaking as though the knowledge of the medical ages belonged to him alone and was not a particularly heavy burden. But the

26

STAINED GLASS: PUTTING THE PIECES TOGETHER

*words burdened me: epilepsy, petite-mal seizures, brain dys-
function, learning disability. "We do not believe he will be a
vegetable . . ."*

*As Mark grew, so did his problems manifest themselves.
Nothing worked correctly on his body. His eyes were crossed. His
ears were plugged with thick fluids. The inside of his mouth was
malformed. As I would try to nurse him in a rocker, his little body
would shake and quiver with intermittent spasms. His lips would
turn purple and my milk would spill from his tongue onto my
breasts. My "perfect" world crumbled. I could no longer hide
behind my masks of propriety. For many months I balanced on
the edge of mixed emotions: "I could reject this child if I choose."
Instead, I slowly became his friend, learning that out of weakness
comes strength. Ever since that time, I would be drawn toward
the seemingly misbegotten and dispossessed.*

*My love for Mark is now bold. He and I have marched
through the years like soldiers in muddy foxholes, from doctor to
doctor, treatment to treatment, surgery to surgery. Mark can now
see, hear, and speak well. He has braces fixing his mouth. At 14,
his hands tremble ever so slightly, but he is seizure-free. He is at
home right now, getting ready for a speaking role in his junior
high school play. His costume is red . . .*

Finally, I'm off the freeway, turning onto Sixth Street. I
see a woman on a corner in a tweed suit and with a brief case. A
little further away, there is a woman dressed in bedroom slippers
and rags, pushing a shopping basket full of aluminum cans. A
light turns, signaling "stop," and I drift inward to a desert of
memories.

*SHANNON and HEATHER. My daughters. My mirrors.
My friendly enemies, challenging me to full womanhood. They*

27

have accepted my gross parental inadequacies and healed me with their presence. Yesterday, the three of us were perched on a grassy cliff above the ocean. Shannon, 11, semi-consciously tugged at her first bra. "Sometimes it's a nuisance growing up, Mom." She is of the earth and doesn't resist its weight. She told me in confidence that she can't wait to start her "period." I read her a poem from a book: "You can melt, and if you do, streams will flow from you to give life and renew the earth."

Heather sat nearby, dangling skinny nine-year-old legs off the cliff, tackling an Abba Zabba bar between her teeth. On her right, her Cabbage Patch Doll, a gift of a relative, and in the world of little girls, the ultimate status symbol. On her left, her one-eyed, scraggly, old stuffed Pink Panther, who protects her through scary dark nights but who holds no social standing in the eyes of her friends. Heather's hair reflected back the pale yellow of the afternoon sun. She had dressed herself in shorts and cotton shirt, but her shiny black patent leather shoes gave away her tiny vanities. I smile, recognizing myself in her. For all my self-induced transformations in the direction of the poor, the oppressed, the homeless, I still refuse to let go of certain symbols of worldliness. Nail polish! I must have my toes magenta or crimson or pink at least. I must have my hair in permanent waves. And my books! I digest them voraciously, then hoard them on shelves like a miser her gold.

The girls brought me a gift from the seaside at the end of our day together—wild mustard flowers. The green stems reflect Shannon who is resilient like grass in the wind. The yellow blossoms are like Heather—bright, warm, free, spontaneous, but with a touch of pride . . .

I pull up to the curb on Gladys Street. The question,

28

STAINED GLASS: PUTTING THE PIECES TOGETHER

"What about the children?" is still in me, unanswered, and I inhale it and exhale it like a non-smoker trying out a cigarette. I see the face of Christ painted on the outside wall of the Catholic Worker Kitchen. The street men are already lined up, waiting for a meal in the lostness of their individual gravities that hold them down on the Row.

Looking inward, I see my own life, for the moment, in shades of gray. Like the street and sidewalk before me. Like the salvage of a shipwreck. Like the shadows cast by the men in front of me. Like the amniotic fluid that pours out of a woman's womb just before she gives birth. Like the fog on a beachfront. I sit in my car and grope inside my heart for answers, but little is tangible, except for the love I feel for my children and my desire to work here in the inner city with the poor. Otherwise, I am a mist of contradiction, filled with confused thoughts that cannot be thought to their end.

My introspection is bordering on maudlin as a kitchen volunteer pokes his head out of the door and waves, "Come on in!" I get out of the car and lock the door. The odor of onions wafts through the air—I didn't escape the sacrificial chore of onion-chopping! I laugh a little and my mind clears. I realize I have been struggling over the wrong question. I already know that *what* I am going to do "about the children" is to move them back to L.A. with me. The real questions remaining are: How do I want to live my life, how do I want to love my children, and what legacy do I want to leave them?

The Catholic Worker philosophy comes close to answering those questions for me. I've been around the Los Angeles Worker long enough to know that the community has its fair share of struggles and flaws. Yet I know as well that I want to be a part of their effort to serve those persons society has forgotten or rejected and to bring some sort of sanity back into a world grown fearful and callous. I know I want to raise my children to be sensitive and aware enough of others to eventually make their own responsible choices beyond mere immediate gratification.

The one and only Gandhi quote I have ever memorized crystallizes before me: "Whenever you are in doubt or when the self becomes too much with you, try the following expedient—recall the face of the poorest and most helpless person you have ever seen and ask yourself if the step you contemplate is going to be of any use to that person...Then you will find your doubts and your self melting away."

With that in mind, I step inside the kitchen and confront the awaiting sack of onions.

BOOK 2
ENCOUNTERS

Even in the most intense activity,
this feeling of unreality—
in me who has never come "close"
to another. The old fairy-tale:
the one who has been made
invisible or transformed into
a beast can only regain his human
shape through someone else's love.

—Dag Hammarskjold

RETURN OF THE MAGI

y first business trip to the State Capitol should have been exciting—touring the newly refurbished Capitol Building; attending lots of important workshops in my executive tweed jacket, leather briefcase appropriately in hand, seeking out the local "hot spots" in town after sunset. The problem was that I had to walk along the K-Street Mall each morning and evening. Serving as the main pedestrian walkway to and from the convention center, it was a trouble-some route for me because its trees, benches, and fountains also served as resting posts for dozens of winos and assorted street people. I pretended indifference, but it irritated me to be rushing by in my best suit while they were sitting or lying there in varying degrees of deterioration, with wine bottles thinly disguised as "acceptable beverages" in brown paper bags.

If I could have claimed ignorance of the streets and those who inhabit them, my attitude might have been more under standable. The truth was that, on innumerable weekends over the years in Los Angeles, I had helped serve meals to men just like these at the Catholic Worker Hospitality Kitchen on Skid Row. Having never been very comfortable with closeness, it had seemed relatively safe serving food to people across a kitchen counter; and with my talent for selective compassion, I had chosen that arena for my acts of mercy. Good works proved one's worthiness and shaved off points in purgatory—a semi-conscious belief left over from the remnants of "old school" Catholicism. Now, with cynical sophistication, I was brushing mercy aside on my way to and from "relevant business" in Sacramento. Though not possessing the perverted depth and character of a Jekyl-Hyde, I was beginning to feel less than human—a sort of plastic-hearted Barbie Doll playing politics in an artificial world. I almost despised these street people because attempting to ignore them hadn't fully insulated me from my guilt.

So, it wasn't a sudden urge for contemplation or a dose of Sanctifying Grace that drew me inside of a Catholic cathedral on my last day in the city. It was simply that I needed a sanctuary from the street and from my own conscience. My first thought as I became aware of the raggedy old man in a corner of the church was, "Damn, I can't get away from them!" He was hovering over a statue of the Infant Jesus of Prague—a rather odd-looking little man, shabbily dressed, a bit stooped with age, white-whiskered and wearing a moth-eaten wool beret tilted slightly over his left ear. I sat rigidly watching him from another corner as though he were about to assault me. Soon, however, I was caught up in an experience that mesmerized me into a kind of timeless suspension.

RETURN OF THE MAGI

Cap tucked under his arm, the man actually began talking to the Infant of Prague! "Hello, my little one...it is me, Pedro...I am a little one too...remember me?...ahh, you are a fine boy...you are full of love..." My face was flushing—I could feel my own warm blood pulsating up my neck, around my temples. It was as though I had intruded on an intimacy of the deepest form. I wanted to run outside, but I was frozen to the pew. My legs might as well have been jello sticks. I was afraid to breathe for fear of interrupting the delicate communicative threads of this man with his Infant friend.

Still entranced, I watched with disbelief as Pedro left the statue and shuffled—in shoes far too big for his feet—up the steps that led to the altar. What was he going to do—desecrate the Blessed Sacrament? Perhaps he was dangerously demented. Perhaps he would freak out and begin to throw candlesticks through windows. Even so, I was compelled to sit there, absorbing every detail.

What he did was like a dance—a sacred dance. He genuflected, rose, circled around, tapped the tabernacle gently, whispered, "My Lord and my God," then began the ritual over. And again. And still again. He cast soft shadows across the floor and I followed his repetitive movements with my eyes, kept his rhythm with my heartbeats, until his prayer became my prayer. After a while, nothing this man said or did seemed eccentric.

Once more, he stood before the Infant of Prague. He was crying. Gentle, quiet tears fell from his face onto the marble floor. Pedro encircled the Infant with his arms. "Hug me," he whispered, "hug me tight." By now I had my own tears to contend with, and my heart was caught in my throat like a fish bone. What kind of world was this where a man is so hungry for

33

tenderness that he must substitute the cold touch of a plaster baby in jeweled cape and crown for the warmth of a human embrace? I was desperately pleading with my own cynicism and doubt to bear a loving God into this world—this church—this statue. God! Please exist and please give Pedro a little love.

He turned and caught my eye. Like Eve in the Garden, I felt "found out" and ashamed. The audacity of earlier pretensions—nose in the air, swinging my briefcase along a street where others were barely able to stay in the swing of survival— my bite from the apple. Pedro began walking down the aisle and in the moment it took him to reach me, my self-consciousness reached overwhelmingly painful heights. Why! Why this distress over coming so close to the guilelessness of an unmasked soul?

I had this ridiculous impulse to strike my breast like I used to as a little girl before receiving Communion. *Lord, I am not worthy*...without words, Pedro took my hand...*To receive you*...without words, we began to hug each other...*Only say the word*..."I love you," he said...*And I shall be healed*..."I love you too Pedro."

After what seemed like a very long time, he let go of me, the scent of old wine lingering on my clothes like myrrh from the Magi. Shuffling out through the huge church door and back onto the K-Street Mall, Pedro disappeared into anonymity. I was left behind with the Infant of Prague, striking my breast to the rhythm of Pedro's sacred dance.

THE BODY OF CHRIST BROKEN FOR US

hey sat down on exotic fan-backed rattan chairs at the table next to mine, four men in business suits, crossing their legs carefully so as not to wrinkle the creases in their pants. It struck me as funny that they all had on the same kind of shoes: black oxfords, tidily laced, well-heeled, with a sheen so smooth I could see my own reflection in each leather upper. We were in a cafe called The Casablanca, inside of a well-established hotel in downtown Pasadena. Ceiling fans circled lazily above walls decorated with tropical-posh floral paper. Tall green palms hung in clay pots everywhere. Humphrey Bogart would have felt at home. I myself felt rather uneasy, having been sent to the hotel by my employer for a weekend conference. The only thing on the menu I could afford to order was the Cream of Wheat. But I ordered it with style.

My weakness whenever I'm alone in a public place is eavesdropping. The prospects didn't seem too promising for any CIA-type secrets to leak out from the four men next to me as they ordered expensive breakfasts. I remained relatively indifferent to their conversation until I heard one of them say "...the Body of Christ..." What's this? Who were these guys? As my ears tuned in and out, I picked up fragments of a fascinating dialogue: "...the Body of Christ is big but we can make it bigger...expansive use of media...proper equipment...a nationwide network of expensive resources to reach a growing audience...build high-tech offices...lots of computer support...create a T.V. spot, a remote church setting, something in stucco or wood... video training rooms for preachers...a cash register on wheels could also serve as a podium...with enough capital, we could have the latest, the hottest, the best information on Jesus available...our Executive Pastor has a specialty field..."

My Cream of Wheat was cold. So was I. Had I heard all of that correctly? Was the Body of Christ being marketed in the dining room of this pretigious hotel? Was it being packaged and wrapped in glittering generalities over a $10.00 per person steak and egg breakfast? These questions haunted me as I paid my bill, ran down the hall to my room, changed into a pair of jeans, then circled through the lobby to my car. I needed to go someplace where I could think more clearly about what I had just overheard.

It took only 15 minutes to reach the house on Skid Row belonging to the Missionary Brothers of Charity, yet it felt as though I were entering another world. The Brothers were old friends of mine and I knew I would be welcome—even be offered a room where I could seek some solitude. But when they greeted me at the door, I felt tense. Not wanting to be alone I asked for some work to do. "As a matter of fact, we need your help with a woman who has been injured..."

The woman was dressed in an unironed sleeveless cotton shift. It startled me when I realized that she had no arms below what should have been elbows, giving the absurd appearance of two sausage links hanging loosely from her shoulders. Her hair fell drab and oily from her head in matted tangles. Small nondescript eyes peered out at me from above huge dark semicircular rings of fatigue. She reeked of perspiration, stale tobacco, and menstrual blood. When she spoke, it was with a slow deliberate sing-song rhythm, leading me to speculate that she might be minimally mentally retarded.

"I need a shower...rape. I was raped. I tried to run away...really...even lost my shoes running fast...they fell off and he caught me. He hurt me. I need a shower." I was struck dumb. Looking down at her bruised scraped feet, I felt helpless and awkward. I motioned for her to follow me to the bathroom. Finding my voice in a corner of my throat, cowering behind my emotions, I "ahemed" and finally spoke. We exchanged names. Hers was Mary. She lived in no particular place and couldn't remember her exact age. "You be my hands, please."

This simple request echoed something from my past days in parochial elementary school. The nuns had a phrase: "The Body of Christ has no hands but yours." I took her clothes off carefully, gently. The odors overwhelmed me to the point of nausea. She was bleeding between her legs. "He hurt me," she reiterated matter-of-factly.

I tried to be tender and took my time with the bath ritual—lathering her body with soap, her hair with baby shampoo, rinsing her all over with lots of warm water. She was submissively patient with my clumsiness. Her breasts were etched with deep scratches and my hand trembled as I washed them. Patting her dry with a terry towel, we chatted a bit. She said she wanted a haircut. I gave her the works—combing, trimming, styling as best I could and tying two pink bows in her hair that my daughter had absent-mindedly plopped in my purse a couple of days earlier. When I had finished, her hair shone splendidly and the ribbons caressed her ears. She looked quite lovely.

The Brothers had discreetly left some sanitary pads, deodorant, powder, and fresh clean clothes outside the bathroom door. Mary selected a blouse and skirt. She wanted a long-sleeved sweater as well so that "nobody knows I still got no arms." She also still had no shoes. Images of the men at the breakfast table with their shiny black oxfords, and visions of my own well-stocked shoe rack at home floated through my mind, seared through my conscience. I knew I had two pair of boots tucked away in the closet back at the hotel. Slowly, I bent down, untied and removed my Nike Runners. Mary tried them on and they fit fairly well. She seemed pleased, much like a child receiving a new toy. Her eyes grew a little misty and so did my own. I hugged her and felt the stubs of her upper-arms attempt an embrace. It said everything. The Brothers treated us both to a warm lunch before I left for Pasadena.

Next morning, having no desire to return to the Casablanca Cafe, I flipped on the color T.V. in my room. It was Sunday and there was a gray-templed, clean-shaven man on the screen wearing a three-piece suit with a white carnation in the lapel, and lots of gold jewelry on his fingers and wrists. He was standing behind a podium. "Friends of Jesus," his voice boomed out, "bring your dollars and stand before the Cross . . ." I turned the sound all the way down, watching his mouth as it silently rolled on and on and on.

I don't know how well-developed my own spiritual life has become—sometimes I fear it is pretty infantile—but I just

THE BODY OF CHRIST BROKEN FOR US

can't grasp a Jesus who can be marketed on a weekly television show, sandwiched in between the praises of Rolaids and the glory of Ivory Liquid. I need to smell the Blood of Christ dripping from the Cross, touch the wounds with my own hands. I long for intimacy and communion, not for multi-media mass merchandising. As I sat there alone in that room staring at the man on the set, I knew that for me the Body of Christ had been crucified barefoot only the day before; had been resurrected in a steamy shower stall that same afternoon; and probably at this very moment—far from the eye of any T.V. camera—was walking in obscurity through the streets of L.A. in a pair of size 7 1/2 blue and gray Nike Runners.

NO ROOM IN THE INN

he sign reads "Public Park" though one would never guess it by the size of its enormous wrought iron entrance gates and the way it nestles so privately in the center of a circle of exclusive sprawling ranch-style homes. Last Fourth of July, I spent the entire afternoon and evening there, not because I wanted to show off my talent on the tennis courts (I can't even hold a racket!), or sip lemonade under an umbrella in the clubhouse patio. Nor was it because of any overwhelming sense of patriotism, although I have gotten teary-eyed watching James Cagney sing and dance to all those George M. Cohan songs on the late late show. It's just that this particular park is THE PLACE in the L.A. area for July Fourth fireworks on a spectacular scale, and I'm a sucker for Starbursts and Whistlers and Moon-Rockets.

Arriving early at the park, I realized I was in trouble when I reached the grassy picnic area, a basket of Kentucky Colonel in my hand. It was crowded and these folks had a weird idea of the definition of the word "public." Individual families—dressed mostly in appropriate white shorts with coordinating red or blue

41

Izod polo shirts—were busying themselves with ropes, stakes, hammers, constructing mini-fortresses around each picnic table. Within the barriers, hoisted alongside miniature American flags, were distinguishing banners, each declaring THE FAMILY NAME.

Would it be an act of civil disobedience if I stepped over these mazes of ropes and flags to try and find an unclaimed patch of grass for myself? I felt like an alien contemplating trespassing and chose instead to walk completely around the edge of the grounds. Finding a little space to spread my blanket out, I tried to act nonchalant, munching my chicken discreetly while two women, safe in their "Smith Headquarters" cubicle, chattered about devising ways for their maids to prepare Peking Duck with a minimum of fuss—something to do with the way one pieces up the ginger root. Feeling a bit vulnerable and out of place, I suddenly found myself wishing that I too had some way of isolating "my area" from the others. I began bordering the blanket I had brought with *my* purse, *my* sweater, *my* lunch basket—anything to indicate "private property."

The sun began to disappear and I settled back to watch the fireworks like a hungry glutton in anticipation of a feast. It was a slick show, and I enjoyed every morsel of the sparkle and dazzle. When it was over, another show began, even more amazing. People were complaining as they reluctantly unfettered their holiday strongholds of twine. A bald man in bermuda shorts grumbled to his fellow companions, "I want a bigger space next year. Maybe I ought to invest in some modern security control equipment to protect my spot." "Yeah," chuckled another, "or rent a killer Doberman from the Canine Behavior Center." They all laughed in unison.

NO ROOM IN THE INN

That was last summer. The days are colder now and I am far away from L.A., living in my home near another more rustic park. Often on walks through the park, I have noticed a scrubby little lean-to hidden in the aromatic luciousness of a cluster of Eucalyptus trees. Yesterday, I spotted a police car there, red lights blinking ominously. Approaching the scene, I saw a tattered middle-aged man standing before two uniformed patrolmen, a younger, pregnant woman beside him. "Ain't no fair we can't stay here. We don't bother no one. We got nowhere else to go. I'm lookin' for work—my wife's gonna have a baby at Christmas time. I built this here place for her and the child. Ain't no fair."

With a sweep of an arm, one policeman demolished the fragile lean-to, it being nothing more than heavy duty trash can liners and sticks. The woman placed her hands across her ripening belly and wailed. The man swore and set his jaw in icy restraint. They were shuffled away into the police car.

I walked gingerly up to the fallen shelter and lifted the plastic covering. No killer Dobermans here. All I found was a pair of old sleeping bags, some stale bread, a jar of jam—two people's meager possessions representing basic survival. And in one corner— a cradle, roughly carved from cheap lumber.

It's a long way from the sophisticated L.A. park to these Eucalyptus trees. It's a long time from the Fourth of July to Christmas. But the same old universal story continues to unfold. There are those of us who in fear draw lines, claim territory, guard our possessions against intruders, divide ourselves one against the other, crave greedily for "more," say "This is mine and not yours." And there are those who are always denied a room in the Inn; who must live peculiarly exposed lives, on the

43

margins of society, with no guarded terrain, no flags of identity—propertyless paupers lost in a sea of the self-contained.

In vain, I tried to re-establish the couple's feeble enclosure with a few broken sticks, pondering for a moment my own house with its locks and fences; my own heart with its protective compartments. I bent over the empty cradle, rocking it to and fro. Away in a manger, no crib for His bed again this Christmas.

Still Christ will be born into this boundaried world with His limitless Love as He has done for centuries—His infant hands reaching across borders, through prison bars, over barbed wire, into trenches, around walls, under barricades, behind curtains, above the nuclear arms build-up, in dirty alleys—stretching out renewed Hope for the hard-hearted and the broken-hearted.

Gently, I folded the tarp back over the cradle. Maybe next winter our Inns won't be so full.

BLUE CHRISTMAS

t's the First Sunday of Advent and, as the hospital chapel fills up with patients, I sit wondering why I chose to work in this kind of place. The room is a blur of blandness, with men in creased khakis taking seats among the straight rows of beige metal chairs or leaning against colorless walls. My eyes feast on the only source of vivid color available—a painting (done long ago by a patient) of St. Dymphna, the patron saint of the mentally ill. I have absolutely no memory of her appearing in my parochial school "Book of Saints," but her likeness is vibrant and alive here, contrasting the institutional pallor with hues of magenta and crimson.

Outside in the hallway, the odor of disinfectant mingles with cigarette smoke and filters into the chapel. Someone opens a window and I notice the window-bars casting a criss-cross shadow along the floor boards, a jolting reminder that I am inside a maximum security facility for the criminally insane.

The man sitting in front of me begins to rock back and forth, holding his head between two trembling hands, moaning unintelligible sounds. I wonder if he is soothing his misery or escalating himself into a state of rage. Nothing is predictable here. Will the man start screaming uncontrollably? Throwing chairs? Will he suddenly make a fist hitting the nearest human target, which in this instance would be me? I feel a tightness in my gut and recognize that I am becoming afraid. I try to hold fast to the belief I carried with me on my first day of work as a psychiatric technician: that the only genuinely lasting way to heal mental illness, short of Divine Intervention, is through human compassion. But fear prompts me to rely more heavily on the accessibility of hospital "artillery" than the dubious strength of my personal caring.

I think about the armaments stockpiled upstairs for this patient: hypodermic needles, pills, tablets, capsules, leather wrist and ankle restraints, the nursing procedure manual full of rules and regulations written for the purpose of maintaining rigid control over this man's behavior. The most pertinent weapon is in my pocket—the keys that open and close every entrance and exit to everywhere this man may ever go while confined here. He begins to calm himself down and, for an instant, I feel my own adrenalin rushing through me, a reminder of how easily I am tempted by the false sense of security and power such authority over another can produce.

The altar server announces the beginning of the Christmas Season and Mass begins. *In the name of the Father*... I'm the only woman present. The room is full of men—a priest, two male nurses, 50 or 60 of the total 1200 committed population who "nutted up on the outside" as they themselves put it, and acted out violently against society. Murderers, rapists, child molesters—they're all present and counted.

And of the Son...I get so confused working here. One

46

minute, the differences between myself and the patients seems enormous; the next minute, microscopic. I look inward at my own stubborn refusal to let go of the memory of past wounds inflicted on me as a child, reflecting on the subsequent destructive patterns I have taken on. I see the moments of betrayal, manipulation, and rejection that I am accountable for, along with all the promises I have been unable to keep. Bloodless and bruiseless actions, tidily and legally dealt with, and therefore I am declared "innocent and sane" by societal standards.

It occurs to me that I am carrying subtler symptoms of the same disease as these patients. I can hardly dwell on that so I diffuse the thought by generalizing with questions: Are the acts of these men *inhuman* or are they manifestations of the dark, and very human side of our nature? Are their deeds compartmentalized perversions or are they intricately woven in with the whole of our actions as human beings?

And of the Holy Spirit...It is so much safer to keep separating "them" from me. It is certainly my tendency to look at myself as a creature of light bearing a few idiosyncratic, but acceptable, weaknesses. But to look at myself as an inheritor of the Fall, breeding character defects that crawl around like maggots in the shadowy corners and crevices of my being, mingling with my holier aspirations, eating away at the goodness in my soul, playing tug-o-war with my integrity—that I cannot bear to view in its full ugliness.

Amen...Better to sit here praying Mass, wearing my professional I.D. badge that segregates me from the Criminal Crazies. The priest asks for petitions and I refocus my attention as the men shift in their seats, clearing their throats.

"I pray I do O.K. when I go back to court." *Lord, hear our prayer.* "I pray for my victims." *Lord, hear our prayer.* "I'm sorry I killed her." *Lord . . .* "Make the voices get out of my head and leave me alone." *Lord . . .*

An interruption from someone in the back row. "Watch out, Father! The trip-wire is just ahead. . .quick, a grenade!" I turn around to see a familiar patient crouching behind his chair, eyes wide with terror. He's flashing back to Vietnam again as he has been doing for several days. A male nurse escorts him into the hall, talking with him gently, bringing him out of the "jungle." It is all over so quickly, I find myself trying to act as though the incident hadn't occurred, folding my hands prayerfully, focusing my eyes on the altar, breathing normally. How else can I compensate for ghosts from a war that technically ended years ago? Father whispers, "Lord, hear our prayer."

I am grateful for Communion. The wafer on my tongue cracks, dissolves, becomes one with the rest of me. I bow my head, closing my eyes as someone's soft tenor voice floats around the chapel.

Lord, don't let me stray too far from Calvary I won't forget you hung between two common criminals for me . . .

The song seems out of sync with the season of Advent. Outside in the streets, people are buying Christmas trees for the kids and ties for Uncle Harry. At this moment in other churches, choir members are most likely practicing "Away in a Manger." But in here, things are a liturgical mess. Christ has already been handed over for 30 pieces of silver and the thieves are carrying their crosses and crying and dying on this forgotten Golgotha hill in California.

The priest turns to us and bids us to "Go in Peace." A black man with massive shoulders and scars across his wrists turns to me, confessing, "I can't go nowhere in no kind of peace till I gets my Thorazine pill." Inexplicably, the knot in my stomach loosens and I am released from my fears. My hand stretches lightly across one of his huge shoulders and we walk out together. I lock the door behind, passing a security guard who waves and nods as we begin to shuffle along with the others down the long dark corridor leading to our "home" ward.

Somebody's radio is playing Elvis Presley's rendition of "Blue Christmas." The appropriateness of that song echoing down this particular hallway causes me to smile. It's the First Sunday of Advent and five minutes before medication line-up. Lord, don't let me stray too far from Calvary.

CUL-DE-SACS OF CONSCIENCE

Even now, the memory rises before me like the shadowy episode of a bad dream. It was a hot summer day. People sat outside on stools or stood against the patio walls of Big Dean's Place on the boardwalk near the Santa Monica Pier, unwinding themselves in the sunshine and sea air by pouring mugs of foamy beer into their bellies. Young kids rock-and-rolled by on their skates, boasting irridescent Pac-Man shoelaces, their arms embracing silver-streamed "ghetto blasters'" blaring out dissonant New Wave sounds. The ancient carousel—housed across the way in its decaying brick, mortar, cinder block castle—competed with the radio noises, its haunting chimes sifting through the broken glass of old windows while the painted ponies circled round and round and round.

It was into this setting that the stranger materialized before me like an apparition, as I cozied myself contentedly on a bench outside of Big Dean's, guiding my tongue along the smooth seductive swirls of my ice cream cone. He looked weary, as though he had come a long way. He was not an old man, but his hair was gray under the sheepskin cap—the long, tangled, filthy hair of a nomadic derelict. Dried mud caked along the edges of his tattered coat. His shoeless feet were swaddled in layers of muslin sheet-strippings, rag-tag replicas of a matchless pair of socks.

I couldn't help staring at this forlorn real-life version of a Dickensian character, but when he stared back, it was all I could do to keep from shielding my eyes as protection against the starving, vacant look in his. To diffuse my embarrassment, I spread a stupid grin across my face, like butter over a hot biscuit. The stranger passed me by, apparently unfed by my smile. He approached the garbage bin which stood like an eyesore over to the side of Big Dean's. A few drinkers shifted uncomfortably on their stools as the man lifted the bin's metal lid, allowing a tactical corps of fat, gluttonous flies to escape.

Feeling nothing more than a mild curiosity, I continued to watch the man, my ice cream melting into a gooey mound on my cone. He scrounged through the bin silently, methodically, an expert technician in the field of trashing.

Then it happened. An aproned bartender ran out, his sweating arms bulging firm tan muscles. "Get outta here, you son-of-a-bitch! Go back to Skid Row where you belong. We don't need scum like you bothering the customers." I was no more than three feet away. Cringing, I said nothing...did nothing. The man merely whispered a faint reply, "I'm hungry," and continued his search through the garbage.

Lunging forward without a warning, the bartender grabbed the dumpster lid with both sinewy arms and in one grotesque, violent gesture, slammed it down on the fingers of the man. To this day I can hear the ghastly wail erupting from the man's throat, tangling with the echo of the lid as it went crashing down, metal on bone. Still, I did nothing. I said nothing. I felt like a prisoner, trapped inside of my own moral paralysis.

Execution accomplished, the bartender returned victoriously to his counter, the drinkers shifted back into position on their stools; and the stranger, holding his hands up like fragile pieces of cracked fine china, shuffled on without retaliation, his eyes now exquisite with pain.

I watched him walk away, sure that his knuckles were broken. Steamy tears filled my own eyes. I thought about calling out, running after him; offering him my handkerchief to bind his wounds; my ice cream as consolation for an empty stomach; a bus token for travel to an emergency hospital. But instead, I sat on my bench speechless, motionless, until the pathetic figure dissolved into the indifference of the beach crowd.

Once, since that time, I returned to sit on the bench next to Big Dean's Place. The walls and windows housing the carousel were newly refurbished. I sat for hours searching the hustling throngs of beach goers and fishermen, looking in vain for that one unforgettable apparition. I glanced shamefully over at the dumpster, recalling mangled fingers. My mind turned over question after question like the leaves of a book blowing in the wind.

What dark side of myself did I encounter that hot summer day? What in my human nature turned my usually warm, healthy heart into rancid chicken liver? Why, witnessing an injustice, did I not act in some way to prevent such a violent, degrading incident? Where was my soul that afternoon, if not cowering in the shadows of a crucifixion, denying the Christ in a threadbare ragman? How can I forgive myself for committing such a gross withholding of love? Will I show more courage the next time... and the next?

I found little solace in inflicting this interrogation upon myself except to conclude that in order to evoke inner change, I must be determined to ask such questions of myself—to confront my own shadow side.

Indeed, as I painfully discovered, there are puny dark dead-end rows inside of me and I have stumbled blindly through at least one of them, bumping up against the different ways to execute people caught within the Big Rows. It can be done all at once on Death Row with an electric current jolting their entire body, or little by little on Skid Row with a dumpster lid cracking knuckles and bones; or it can be done at every cul-de-sac of conscience with our apathy, indifference, moral paralysis.

It takes a lot of personal confronting to crawl out of the shadows of our interior rows where we are tempted to hide, and out into the light of God's grace where we can move in the active direction of love and justice.

If I had ignored my sins the Lord would not have listened to me. But God has indeed heard me. He has listened to my prayer.

—Psalm 66:18-19

LOVING TOO MUCH: ENCOUNTERS WITH
A PROSTITUTE AND A SAINT

I'll admit it. Last year my personal relationships were in a shambles. It was during one of those post-earthquake rainy days in Southern California that I waded into a funky little bookstore along the Venice Boardwalk looking for a book that would cure all my intimacy hang-ups.

I was already late for work and had used up a half-hour searching for the "perfect" literary antidote for my relationship woes. Finally, I drifted over to the biography section where a biographical work about Dorothy Day caught my eye. Then, on a nearby shelf, I saw *it*...the ultimate relationship guide for women! You tend to remember a book title when half a dozen of your closest women friends call you up one by one, all saying the same thing: "Gee, Toni, I just finished reading *Women Who Love Too Much* and wow...it really reminded me of you!"

The rain poured down outside. I had to get to work, so I decided to purchase the copy of Dorothy's biography. A few drops plopped from the leaky ceiling onto the paperback bestseller *Women Who...*etc. I picked up that book too. One friend had jokingly referred to it as "294 pages of Toni's love life." Remembering this, I promptly purchased it, along with the Dorothy Day book, just to read it and prove my friend wrong.

My work assignment that day was at the Santa Monica Jail where I counsel homeless people who are without resources. The woman I saw there had spent the night in a cell. Her clothes were wrinkled, her body was infused with grime. She was devoid of even one singularly winning physical characteristic. Slumped shoulders announced fatigue; wide eyes hinted contradictions of defiance and regret. Lifting a trembling hand to her head, tangled fingers met with matted hair performing twisted rituals, diffusing nervous exhaustion. She stared at me and said flatly, "Stay away...I smell like old armpit and stale booze!"

A jailer handed me her police report, the door swung closed with a heavy vibrating sound of metal on metal. The woman swooped a hand compulsively across her sweater, lifting it up and down, revealing stomach flesh. The jailer said, "This isn't the way to behave..." to which she retorted with a fierce, tattered dignity, "It's how *I* behave!" The police report described her as 35 years old, occupation "laborer." The jailers identified her as "...probably a prostitute." Whatever her profession, it looked to me like she'd done years of hard labor. If her body was her source of income, she appeared to have given far more than she'd been paid for in recent times.

Her crime was "lewd conduct." The arrest report spelled out in exacerbatingly intricate, indelicate detail the precise nature of her offense; how she had shouted obscenities whilst waving bare buttox and breasts at some passers-by in an outdoor shopping mall and then enthusiastically repeated the performance for the cop-on-the-beat. (He later must have written up the account with a burning pen, as every indiscreet nuance of the woman's actions could be read animatedly on the police sheet.)

Holy God! I experienced an initial reaction of puritanical indignation toward the woman. How could she degrade herself so...embarrass and insult people trying to shop? But then I began thinking about how worn-down and worn-out she looked. And how many times in my life I'd felt worn-down and worn-out. I asked, "Haven't you got a home? Anyone I can call for you?" She let out a sob and told me about a "boyfriend" who "lives in a big mansion in Malibu." She's been waiting for months, she says, to move into the house with him. He met her in a bar where he spends time with his buddies. "Sometimes I wish I were a man—I could be his buddy...I waited for him all day at the bar...I got carried away, I guess. Never would have done those things 'cept for too much beer and too much waiting."

She smiled a hollow smile. But I saw her still tugging away sensually at her sweater with all the impulsive passions of a broken woman, avoiding the violence of her hopeless reality. "I don't need help from you. My boyfriend will send for me. Anyway, I can work for a living if I have to..." She seemed caught in that sad state where change is impossible without Divine Intervention, leaving her to become only more of what she already had become. I told her she would be going to court over the charges filed against her and she accepted this fact like someone accepting cream for their coffee. She was, I reflected, so admirably strong in her weaknesses.

Long after I left the jail, the woman remained in my thoughts. Her poverty, pathos, and sexual vulnerability awakened in me an incredible emotion that I had not felt fully until my encounter with her. It was associated, in some way I cannot specifically express, with a sense of having shared a compartment on a train with her through miles of remote wilderness. Personal memories surfaced that I had kept submerged in one of those subconscious anterooms where I store all of the feelings I haven't grown brave enough to explore yet.

Once home, I pulled out the paperback and read the introduction which began, "Women Who Love Too Much... When you keep wishing and hoping he'll change." I set the book down, remembering myself at six years old, hanging out in the kitchen, swigging 7-Up from a beer mug, singing choruses of "When Irish Eyes Are Smiling" with my father and his drinking buddies—dark-eyed, slick-haired Italian Mafia-looking types; nice enough fellows in their own way. How to be my father's pal way my major pre-occupation as a child. By the time I began to memorize my First Holy Communion prayers, I had already mastered the art of swearing in Italian under two forms: words and gestures. And like the woman at the jail, I had learned the art of waiting...for the sound of my father's car late at night, fearing that he might drink too much, get killed in a crash, leave me abandoned.

I have never quite shaken off the desire to be "one of the guys" nor the habit of feeling like I am waiting for...whom? what? Men similar to my father *find* me...or I find them. I've placed myself in some awfully embarrassing predicaments when the waiting for whatever it is we humans long for in our darker, lonelier moments evades me for that one moment more than I can bear. Years of counseling failed to "cure" me altogether of a subdued pervasive sense of longing. Was I after all, merely one of many women who "love too much"? I hoped in my heart of hearts that I was more substantial than the sum total of a few efficiently descriptive remarks printed in a trendy modern pop psychology book.

I read somewhere that we humans want to categorize a diagnosis for ourselves as a relief for our own sense of powerlessness in the face of overwhelming emotions and needs existing both within ourselves and within the world. We try to do "treatment" on our souls, but no x-rays can lay bare the metastatic growth of rage and despair. No biochemical tests of bodily fluids can explain the presence of hopelessness, helplessness, longing. No medicine can serve as an antidote for losses of people, memories, dreams. There are no firm guidelines between abnormality, sickness and sin. Someone else's disturbed behavior is disturbing to us because it is a reminder of our own inability to contain ourselves within certain emotional boundaries.

It was late in the evening when I finally picked up the biography of Dorothy Day, learning incredible "secrets" about her: how she had once lived in Greenwich Village, nursed Eugene O'Neil through the D.T.'s and other terrors of his alcohol-filled nights; how she had experienced at least one hopeless love affair; obtained an abortion; how she had married; how she had later lived with—and loved—her common-law husband and borne him a child.

Merely another "woman who loved too much"? If so, it was out of that same capacity to love "too much" that Dorothy Day converted from Communism to Catholicism, started a radical newspaper, founded the Catholic Worker movement, and devoted the rest of her life moving from daily Mass to wherever there were soup lines for the hungry, picket lines for the sake of justice. She was a living Work of Mercy, a breathing Sign of Peace. She was called by historian David O'Brien, "...the most significant, interesting, and influential person in the history of American Catholicism." She died at age 83 still doing what she had always done—loving foolishly, unreasonably.

So it was that in one 24-hour period, I acquainted myself with two remarkably unforgettable women: a prostitute and a saint. The woman at the jail was one more "fallen woman" in a world where so many of us pick up stones to throw at what is the mirrored image of ourselves, unrecognized. Dorothy Day might also be looked at as a "fallen woman" who transcended her woundedness and her passion into a love of Christ, a zeal for social justice, compassion for the hungry, the poor, the forgotten, and the misbegotten.

I imagined a sort of grace pouring down on me that night, like the rain. For a time I was able to see dimensions of who I am now, reflected in the exquisitely painful presence of the woman isolated behind jail bars and behind her own sexual frailty. I was also able to see the possibilities of what-I-am-not-yet come to life on the pages of Dorothy's biography. By the time *my* 83rd birthday rolls around, I hope that I will have attained redemption and healing, whether in this world or the next. And I hope that my relationship life becomes healthier over the years. But I'm not so sure that I ever want to be "cured" altogether of loving too much.

"...she has anointed my feet with perfume. I tell you, that is why her many sins are forgiven—because of her great love. Little is forgiven the one whose love is small."

—Luke 7:46-47

BOOK 3
BEYOND THE REEF

The seasons
have changed.
And the light.
And the weather.
And the hour.
But it is the
same land.
And I begin to
know the map.
And to get my
bearings.
　　—Dag Hammarskjold

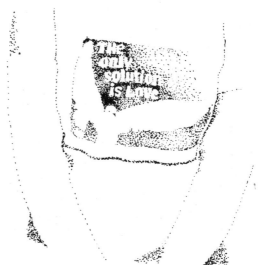

JOURNEY BEYOND THE REEF

oing a civil disobedience action against the Diablo Canyon Nuclear Power Plant started out to be a real sacrifice on my part. The week before the action, everything that could go wrong, did!

At work, two of us were left to staff the responsibilities of a seven-person office. That meant no lunches, lots of over-time. Then my seven-year-old daughter, Heather, came down with a bad case of strep throat. I stayed up each night, rocking her back and forth into the wee hours, soothing her angry fever with cool cloths. My son, Mark, began having problems with his special education class, requiring me to attend early morning meetings with his teachers. My older son, David, grew extremely resentful of the time I spent at nonviolent training sessions and affinity group gatherings. I was over-worked, under-slept, and irritable, but I stubbornly held onto a semi-conscious vision of myself as an activist-oriented combination of wonder woman and earth mother.

Two days before the action, I was doing the evening dishes—completely zombied out. The children began squabbling. The noise level heightened. Something in me snapped. As though possessed, I threw a soapy cup on the floor, then another, and another—six in all. My 10-year-old daughter, Shannon, grabbed my arm, "Please stop, Mom!" Oh God...what a mess! With every cup, I had shattered the images of myself as peaceful resister to the nuclear build-up. I stayed up until dawn, repenting and sweeping up bits of glass. I was forced to acknowledge my limitations.

So much for tangible evidences of sacrifice. I persevered, and when the time arrived for the protest, light broke unexpectedly through the darkness of my struggles. The children grew calm and so did my nerves.

My affinity group numbered four: myself, Edd, Noreen, Mike, plus two guides. Our mission was to penetrate the back hills leading to the nuclear power plant, getting as close as possible to "Badge Alley," a security check-in spot for Diablo workers, very near the reactors.

Having weak ankles and an intense fear of poison oak, I wasn't sure I could make the entire hike of approximately six to ten miles down canyons, up hills. "Step by step," I kept chanting to myself. No prayers, just "step by step"—the coward's liturgy. Earlier, we *had* prayed together, attending noon Mass at the Old Mission Church in our jeans and matching blue shirts with decals defining us as "Waging Peace." Father Simon blessed us, saying, "I am now Father Aloysious Simon, blesser of civil disobedience!"

Beginning at 10:30 p.m., Friday, February 18, we hiked through the hills and into the night for eight hours, stopping only a few times to munch on fruit, sip water, and absorb some of the natural beauty of mountain and sky, around us and above us. And so it was that on my way to being arrested, I came to intimate terms with such lyrical sounding places as the Irish Hills, the English Hills, and Deer Canyon, under the light of a full moon laced delicately with stars. Some poems must be lived, not written, and for that one night, I experienced the exultant poet's life.

The last leg of our journey was spent contouring hills, grappling down a ravine, crawling through a drain pipe underneath the paved road leading into the plant, running through a field of nettles and wild flowers on a cliff overlooking the sea. Restless-sounding waves splashed against rocks, urging us on until we reached the first watch-tower at the edge of the plant. One thing I learned is that it is not difficult to penetrate Diablo. We weren't spotted until we attracted attention to ourselves by walking down the main roadway carrying a huge banner with a logo proclaiming "Light — Life — Love." In fact, we managed to be ignored until we reached the first parking lot inside the plant, about a quarter of a mile from the reactors.

We tried to dialogue during the arrest procedures with the guards, the workers, the sheriffs. Some seemed responsive, others didn't. Nevertheless, we kept talking all the way to the San Luis Obispo County Jail where we were subsequently confined for four days (over a holiday weekend) awaiting our Tuesday arraignment.

Even though I was placed in a cell with nine other protesters—some of whom I knew—it was a difficult four days for me. I guesss I suffered from a claustrophobic feeling of evironmental deprivation. The extreme contrast of experiencing the loveliness of the back country wilderness, only to be locked in an overcrowded cell with no viewable windows, was at times acutely painful. The wild flowers, the rocks, the rich, brown dirt, the aromatic sage, the bubbling streams, the sweet-smelling grass, the sound of the wind caressing the tips of trees, the music

63

of crickets and frogs performing concertos inside the nooks and crevices and secret places hidden in the hills—all of that replaced now by four walls of colorless concrete, a linoleum floor, three steel bunk-beds, four army cots, one toilet, one sink, and a locked door. I reminded myself that this was a small price that I chose to pay for a cause of high value.

I would lie on my back in an upper bunk, staring at the flickering fluorescent light, remembering the moon's glow, moist and feminine, accompanied by the sparkle of the Big Dipper and Orion. I would think of the reverence the members of our affinity group had shown each other in the forest. Then I would re-experience, in my mind, the degradation of the body search—my body exposed and naked, being ordered by a woman guard in uniform to spread my buttocks, then to squat and cough. That will forever remain my Eucharist with all women prisoners.

My eyes grew swollen and red on the second day—some kind of weed allergy. I was taken to the Nurse's Station across the the men's side of the complex. Right across the way was a single cell with a huge green steel door and a small open hole at about my waist level. Above the door was a sign in big red letters reading "No clothes, No blankets, No matches, No cigarettes." As I was reading it, a man's eyes and nose pushed through the hole, startling me. "Oh my God! Someone is in there." I am so naïve. I scanned the sign a second time. Surely he wasn't in there, naked, with not even a blanket? What could he have done? A guard walked by and closed the peephole, blocking the man inside into deeper, darker solitary. The eyedrops stung my eyes when the nurse dropped them in and I was thankful for the release of tears it produced. I returned silently to my cell which suddenly looked to me like a well-lit mansion.

JOURNEY BEYOND THE REEF

On our last day, we had a little "party." The 10 of us had grown quite close. I had never really chosen to associate with clusters of women—always used to migrate into the kitchen with my Dad and his buddies as a child—"one of the boys," he used to call me. But I like women a lot these days. I like being a woman a lot, too. We 10 risked opening up our hearts and spreading some of our secrets out to one another: "My son joined the Marines. I just could not reject him, in spite of my pacifist convictions. So I wore my 'Peace' button and picnicked with him at the Base on 'Parents' Day'"..."I had an abortion once. I was very young. I've spent 20 years trying to reconcile that decision with my nonviolent actions—would that God be a merciful God!"... Courageous revelations from women in touch with the spectrum of human frailty—from nuclear power and weapons to childbirth and the menstrual cycle. Maybe our Father in heaven *is* our Mother after all!

One woman was Hawaiian. She taught us how to do Hawaiian dance—mostly, how to paint pictures of words with our hand movements. We painted this song:

> *Beyond the reef*
> *Where the sea is dark and cold*
> *My love has gone*
> *And my dreams grow old.*
> *There will be no tears, no regret*
> *Will he remember—will he forget?*
> *I send a thousand flowers*
> *Where the trade winds blow*
> *I'll send my lonely heart*
> *For I love him so*
> *Beyond the reef.*

65

The room grew so quiet, each of us seeming to recall at least one great lost love in our life. Then we decided that what was lost here in the shadow of Diablo—and the apparent inevitability of its going on the line—was hope, and that what we were all about here in cell 109 was "going out beyond the reef."

Just then, my name was called out over the speaker system—I had a visitor! I was led to a little plexi-glass cubicle and there was a whole crowd waiting for me! Three friends had brought my children. We were able to talk for an hour. When the hour was up, my youngest girl reached up to the screen that divided us, and through the mesh I touched her hand. Her skin felt so warm. I couldn't help thinking about mothers who are doing regular time—the women and their children are *both* condemned to touching each other through a screen on a window in a cubicle. "I'll see you tomorrow, everyone! Save up the hugs." I had mixed feelings about saying that so certainly when others in the jail could not. But I did indeed see them "tomorrow." I was arraigned, given time served for trespassing, and received a grand welcome home by friends and family.

What had begun as a tedious, draining sacrifice with doubtful fruition, had grown into a gift of disproportionate size. Before the action, I had based my decision to do civil disobedience on obviously justifiable rationalizations. I told my self that as a parent and as a local resident of San Luis Obispo County, I was obligated to act in some strong way to make a statement against Diablo. After all, this particular nuclear power plant had been plopped carelessly by PG&E on an earthquake fault practically in my own back yard, with a history of countless construction and design errors that even the NRC could not ignore.

But deep inside, I struggled with more delicate

66

motivations. The real sacrifical offering was made when I risked following through with a personal conviction in spite of obstacles and in the full light of my own very human flaws. I am still sorting out the peak experiences, the moments of enlightenment, the blessings that tiptoed in with the "sacrifice," uninvited, unexpected. For those who dare to go out beyond the reef...though sometimes dark and cold...a thousand flowers await. I have quite a bouquet.

SUICIDE WATCH IN THE DESERT

he cold January air mingled with the early morning sun and washed over the Nevada desert like watercolor on a canvas. I stood there witnessing the play of light and shadows on the desert rocks, discovering new combinations of colors painted on the sand and fantastic patterns created by various forms of brush and cactus.

I felt overwhelmed by the vastness of the desert and by the pleasurable sensations the environment evoked in me. But accompanying these feelings was a nagging sense of imminent danger. For sometime during the last days of the last month of 1985, a nuclear bomb named Goldstone was exploded 1,800 feet below the desert ground where I now stood. Costing 30 million dollars, the test of the x-ray laser was considered a key element in President Reagan's strategic defense initiative program. The impact of the explosion was reported to be equivalent to as much as 150,000 tons of TNT.

It was the impact of *that* knowledge that called out to me and led me to the Nevada Test Site, along with Thomas Gumbleton—a Catholic auxiliary Bishop of Detroit, some

members of the Franciscan Order, a handful of Los Angeles
Catholic Workers, and over a hundred other "ordinary" people.
We spent the wintery morning of January 3 marking the end of
the six-month Soviet unilateral moratorium on nuclear testing
by praying, singing, vigiling along the main roadway leading into
the site, waving peace banners at the bus-loads of workers
arriving to perform their daily tasks, hoping to bring to their
attention—and to remind the world—that what happens here is
madness.

Later that day, 34 protesters from our weary but spirited
band of desert wanderers were arrested for trespassing on the
Test Site. It was at about that time that I took off my mittens and
lost hope. As I watched the police handcuff my friends with
plastic wrist ties and lead them off to a waiting van, it seemed to
me that what we were doing was so puny in contrast to the miles
of arid flatness stretching out endlessly before us; and in even
more striking contrast, to the depths of the desert floor where
"ordinary" people like us experimented with nuclear bombs.

Suddenly, an unreasonable fear gripped me and the desert
engulfed me and I could no longer see its loveliness. It was a
familiar fear—something I had felt before—somewhere else, but
I could not make the connection. Instead, I looked down at my
feet and my imagination unleashed itself, conjuring up secrets
hidden under the surface of things, huge unslayable monsters
living in dark pits, bleeding their poison sores onto the underside
parts of the earth and inside of people's hearts where no one
could see them and where their evil could be denied. At that
moment, like a child frightened by a nightmare, I wanted to deny
the presence of evil too. I wanted to escape to a slot-machine at
the Four Queens Hotel in nearby Las Vegas where all I had to slay

was a one-armed metal bandit that swallowed up my quarters. Better yet, I wanted to run away to Barstow and overdose on McDonald's burgers and french fries. Forget about Goldstone, just let me walk through the Golden Arches and experience the ignorant bliss of a chocolate shake.

The man next to me at the vigil touched my jacket lightly, "Are you alright?" "Sure...sure, just feeling a little distracted," I replied, wondering if my fear were visible to him. "It's eerie out here," he whispered, "sort of like standing guard over our own suicide attempts." And with that phrase, he hit me over the head with the connection of my fear there in the desert to some unresolved fears experienced in my recent past. It did indeed feel like a suicide watch out there. I should know because in my profession as a mental health worker I had done suicide watches on more than one occasion. My first patient assignment in a psychiatric hospital had been to a suicidal man. He was extremely obese and seemingly docile, but had, by his own admission committed terrible offenses against women. He justified his actions by picking fragmentary phrases out of the Old Testament and saying that God directed him to carry out violence. He boasted about his drug habits, his alcohol abuse, and his various suicide attempts. He was a tormented man.

I, for my part, dutifully set about to "fix" him. Within the hospital setting, I started him on a jogging regime, arranged for a weight reduction diet, took him to Mass on Sundays so that he might interpret God's Word more sanely. I accompanied him to Alcoholics Anonymous and Narcotics Anonymous meetings. My hospital co-workers lauded me for my devotion to this patient and credited me for the positive changes in him. I felt that the praises were well-deserved and I wore them like a jeweled crown.

71

He killed himself on my birthday. I heard the screams of the others as I walked up the stairs leading to the ward. . .saw the vomit and blood oozing from his mouth as he lay on the floor. . . and in his hand, a birthday card addressed to my name. As a nursing team, we worked as hard as we could, doing cardiac massage, clearing his airway, loosening his belt, his shirt, but it was too late. He had hung himself with a sheet. He was gone. I had fixed nothing. Nothing. I opened up the card, halfway expecting to read some insightful suicide message. But he had merely signed his first name and underlined it. I felt shock. Then anger. And finally guilt. Could I have prevented this? Why didn't I see it coming? What did I do wrong? I was reduced to powerlessness.

It was not much different from the powerlessness of standing dwarfed in the desert wilderness, experiencing despair that despite years of my life spent leafletting and protesting, we as human beings had persisted in pushing ourselves to the very brink of collective suicide. Shock. . .anger. . .guilt. Could I help prevent the world from hanging itself with a nuclear rope? Or was I once again going about it all wrong? Certainly, if I could not "fix" one tormented man into wholeness, I could not force the government into changing its military policies or people into changing their thinking about "defense systems" and war. And yet to do nothing. . .

My thoughts drifted back again to the guilt I carried after my patient's death, which did not lift itself off my shoulders, even after I relocated myself in a new psychiatric facility a few months later. I found myself assigned again to do suicide watch over a young adolescent girl. It was then that the guilt diminished and I was overtaken with almost paralyzing fear. After painful discernment, I took the assignment. How can I explain what

72

went differently? I left my ego out of the situation. Whatever fears, worries, personal problems I had, they stayed outside of the locked unit where the young girl lived. Whatever need I had to fix, save, sanctify, adjust or alter another human being, also stayed outside.

I stripped myself down and brought only two things to this child: compassion and intense presence. Her psychiatric profile was as thick as a world history book. She was diagnosed as a psychotic, with auditory and visual hallucinations. It was later discovered that she had a cyst growing inside of her head, wrapping itself around her brain tissue. Every day I would enter her room and be present to her. I would ask very few questions and she rarely spoke to me, except in anger. The hospital rules dictated that I remain at arms length from her at all times and never allow any obstacle to come between us. At first, she would lash out at me, "This is horrible. . . you even watch me go to the bathroom. . . I hate you!. . . I want to die!" She would curl up in a corner of her room like a caterpillar trying to spin into a cocoon, her long dark hair falling over her face concealing impenetrable almond eyes. I, in turn, would curl up alongside the wall, keeping her within reach but recognizing her need for some sort of separateness from me.

Eventually, as time progressed, an intimacy formed between us. The kind that happens when two people experience together, and survive, both madness and the mundane. She began to tell me about her "voices." "I have demons in my head. They dance in there until I get headaches. They have power over me but they protect me too. They keep away the even worse demons. They tell me to hurt myself and I have to obey them." Once she tried to grab scissors from the nurses' station. Another time she reached for a belt. Still another, she tried to pound her fist through a glass window. Each time I would say NO to my fear and NO to her demons. "I hate you," she would say as I put myself between her and whatever object might do her harm. And so we continued day in and day out.

As I witnessed her demons at work in her, I wrestled with my own darkness. There were several temptations. The strongest one was to flee from the situation altogether—to drop myself from the case so that in the event she did take her own life, I would not have to deal with any personal issues. Another was the continual urge to analyze, draw conclusions, and then set about to "change" the girl into a well person. Another temptation was my growing dependence on her "needing" me. One particular day, she demonstrated some relief from the internal stimuli that usually possessed her so completely. I remember feeling, for an instant, a flicker of disappointment that she might be getting better. The final temptation was to become intrigued by her demons. They danced a seductive dance and I had become almost as acquainted with them as she was.

When one is in an intense relationship with another who is ill, it is difficult to love within the context of detachment, where one can simultaneously care for the person and reject their demons. I am more and more convinced, however, that this is one of the most essential ingredients for healing. Somehow, by grace or fortune, I resisted these temptations and in the process, learned the meaning of true heroics from this young girl who in time decided to risk her life in order to save her life by consenting to brain surgery to remove the cyst that was eating away at her. . .

Standing in the desert recalling the details of this girl's

agony and ultimate bravery, my eyes began to be opened again to the beauty of the desert landscape. I continued to make connections between my suicide watch with her and the watch I was doing at the Nevada Test Site. All the processes and all the temptations that happened then seemed pertinent to what was happening in the desert. I began to find the courage to stand firm, in prayerful presence, holding tight my hand-made peace banner. I began to resist the seductiveness of the nuclear dance of destruction. . .saying NO to demons capable of destroying all of life. I began to feel compassion for myself and for everyone in the world while detaching myself from the human thinking that rationalized the "morality" of nuclear weaponry into existence.

Before I left the desert that day, I had come to full terms with the fact that I alone could not expel demons, nuclear or otherwise. It would take both a personal and a collective human change of heart—a willingness to recognize, confront and denounce first our perverted, self-destructive thinking patterns and finally the weapons we have created to fulfill this insane global death wish. It would take a great collective courage to disarm both our minds and our planet. Anais Nin wrote: "I know the origin of war, which is in each of us, and I know that our concept of the hero is outdated, that the modern hero is the one who would be master of his own neurosis so that it would not become universal, who would struggle with his myths, who would know that he himself created them, who would enter the labyrinth and fight the monster. This monster who lives at the bottom of the brain and is projected out."

Thinking back on my day in the desert, and on all the suicidal implications that were represented to me at the Nevada

Test Site, I remember clearly that the more I set aside my own fears and neurosis, the more I began to feel once again the coolness of the desert air on my face and to notice for the first time, purple flowers blooming on some obscure desert weeds.

FINDING MY WAY

sk anyone who knows me well. I'm always tripping over the world around me. At work, the other mental health clinicians shake their heads, saying I have "problems functioning within my external environment." I'm terrified of walking on piers where you look down and see the water lapping between the planks. I'm petrified of riding in outside elevators attached to 10-story buildings by mere cable threads. I lose my car in supermarket parking lots. I walk through the automatic "out" door on my way *in* to the bank. I perpetually misplace my keys, theatre tickets, the book I was reading just before using the bathroom three minutes earlier.

Most irritating to my friends and agonizing to myself is the plain fact that it is next to impossible for me to drive to an unfamiliar destination. I can't read maps. I can't follow directions. "Turn *right* at the *first* intersection, veer *left* at the *north* end of the *second* crossroad after passing through the *southeasterly* section of town"...?! You might as well send me out in search of the Holy Grail—I'm lost at the first right turn, no matter what I'm trying to find.

I have been thinking a lot about my "lostness" in these past few days since the Alliance for Survival's protest action at WINCON—the annual conference between the military and the arms industry. I was there. Along with members of the L.A. Catholic Worker and the Alliance for Survival, I performed an act of what is commonly referred to as "civil disobedience." But more about *what* I did later. Here first is an attempt to explain why someone as awkward and phobic as I am could muster together enough singlemindedness to face a throng of weapons production experts, U.S. Marines in combat fatigues, sheriffs in full uniform, news media, and lines of cars stalled for a mile down the road upon which I stood clutching a scrappy piece of cardboard with the words, "The only security is through Peace."

Taking part in the action was a personal accomplishment for me, yet intimately connected to my brokenness and my past. As a child, I learned to mistrust, in the most traumatic sense, what was for me the "world"—my family and the house where we lived. My childhood environment was chronically violent. I have found, in sharing with others from backgrounds similar to mine, that for those of us who as children have witnessed and/or have been direct targets of violence within our own families, a sort of post-traumatic stress syndrome follows us through our

78

lives. (Some psychologists have noted that it is remarkably similar to the syndrome suffered by war veterans.) As adults, some of us perpetuate the cycle of violence in our own lives because it is what we know best. Others of us spend our whole lives on the run from commitment and from any form of rootedness on the premise that a moving target is less likely to get hit. Still others, like me, retreat inward, trying secretly and solitarily to mend the damage that has been done. We seem to function on the surface reasonably well, but are terrified, really, of the world at large and of those in authority over us.

To this day, I escape to my inner world whenever I feel threatened. As a result, I feel as if my interior life is more developed and reliable than my exterior one. Introspection remains my primary preoccupation. Where I am often clumsy and absent-minded with people, places and events in my physical environment, I feel graceful and illuminated interiorly. I ponder, question, and internalize everything. Sometimes I get carried away and interpret this contemplative ability grandiosely. After all, am I not forging uncharted paths deep inside myself?

But in my more honest moments, I realize that I have not yet achieved an integrated interior life. My thoughts and feelings most often remain buried inside as daydreams and fantasies. My insights generally lie in a state of partial paralysis. To put it bluntly, I am afraid to move outward toward action. On my wall at home, I recently hung a picture of a rose with the quote, "The time came when the risk it took to remain closed in a bud became more painful than the risk it would take to flower."

On February 27 at El Toro Marine Base, the site of WINCON '87, my time for risk was at hand. I don't mean the risk of going to jail. I mean that for me the action was like turning my insides out, exposing to tremendously powerful authority figures that part of me that I have spent years protecting—the part of me that most often, in the past, has withdrawn from the madness rather than chance being swallowed up and consumed by it; that has taken sanctuary within, rather than succumb to the paradoxical temptation of doing violence in opposition to violence and thereby discovering that I have become what I most dread.

At WINCON, I tried to break through these fears in the realization that I am experientially expert in the futility of using violence as a means of bringing about any semblance of authentic lasting peace. Whether the cycle of violence is perpetuated within individuals, families, or nations, it remains both immediately and ultimately destructive. It leads to insanity. It never brings about true security. For the first 18 years of my life, I witnessed daily someone close to me repeatedly build up defenses, break down communication and trust, and act out violently in the name of "gaining control and putting an end to things once and for all." The end never came. No one was ever really in control because the violence became its own entity.

Violence between individuals is a tiny fragment of the collective destruction on the brink of which we find ourselves today. The entity of violence has grown so monstrous that it can now literally destroy all of life. At the El Toro-based WINCON conference, I saw my childhood family situation being re-enacted right before my eyes.

Standing there in the middle of it all, I might as well have been 10 years old again. I felt that powerless. I asked myself, "What will you do this time? Retreat to your inner world?" I prayed to the God that I had found within my soul. I prayed for the courage to act within the context of my own powerlessness. I prayed to believe that God dwelled equally within each person I would confront. And then I went public. As usual, I felt awkward and intimidated, but I managed to step in front of a moving car trying to enter the Base Conference. I held up my cardboard "Peace" sign. The person in the car caught my eyes as a newspaper journalist put a microphone in front of me and said, "Aren't you scared?" I said, "Yes." A sheriff asked me to move. I said, "No." He responded, "You're under arrest for blocking traffic."

I was handcuffed and taken to a bus. The whole thing lasted about 15 minutes. From the bus I could see the sheriff who had just arrested me. I supposed that he thought I had said "no" to his request for me to move. But I knew that my "no" was bigger than he could ever imagine: NO to the entity of violence that had enveloped my childhood and NO to the same entity enveloping the world to this day. For 15 minutes I had stood in the midst of people preparing for insanity and I had not retreated. For 15 minutes, by God's grace, I had disarmed my heart and remained *sane.* The bus started up, made a turn onto a road. I couldn't determine whether it was taking me North, South, East or West, but I knew that I wasn't lost.

AFTERWORD

In the autumn of 1982 I was handed Toni Flynn's first manuscript to critique for possible publication in our Catholic Worker
newspaper, *The Agitator*. It was easy for me then, in my naïvete
as a small-time editor, to casually dismiss her neophyte efforts as
having very little potential. But Toni was determined to become
a bona-fide writer, if only for a tiny contingent of readers in the
peace and justice movement. Over the years, her articles have
progressed to the point where, instead of major cutting and
rewriting, they seldom need any revision. She has evolved into a
moving and insightful journalist, and a number of her writings
have been printed in other publications.

Moreover, there is never a hint in her essays of
triumphalism or holier-than-thou smugness—that bane of the
social activist writer who sees himself or herself as a focal point
for redeeming the world. Her humility and integrity are evident
in her efforts to express her own truth—those real emotions and
experiences that inspire and sometimes haunt her. Throwing a
cup across the kitchen floor (in front of one's children, no less!)
in an attack of pre-civil disobedience jitters is not a very flattering
self-portrait, but I can relate to it. If we are honest about it,
failures such as this occur in all of our lives, but they are balanced
by moments of extraordinary grace. And so, we witness the
morning when Toni gently gives a shower and shampoo to a
homeless and armless woman who had just been raped. In these
instances, and in the other events you have just read about, Toni
doesn't portray herself as having perfect faith or perfect insight,
but remains right there with the rest of us ordinary beings. Yet,

AFTERWORD

we sense that she will never stop striving for greater understanding.

All of this she has accomplished while mothering four children, working a 40-hour week and resisting war and injustice. I myself am a mother of five, and so I know intimately the intensity of her struggle. I have often marveled at the energy and dedication with which she has persisted toward her goal.

Toni's achievement is reassuring to women everywhere who are struggling to attain their own personal dreams— whether it be writing, painting or other creative venture—while remaining faithful to their commitments to children, work, and society.

Joan Trafecanty